"Will God Have a Car Seat for Me in Heaven?"

What our kids' questions teach us about life

by jim maddox

a reflection journal

This book is dedicated to my kids, Michael, David, Kate, and Jake. You have been my greatest joy and blessings. I am so proud of each of you for the young adults you have become.

All Bible quotes are from THE HOLY BIBLE, NEW INTERNATIONAL VERSION®, NIV® Copyright © 1973, 1978, 1984, 2011 by Biblica, Inc.™ Used by permission. All rights reserved worldwide.

Copyright 2017 by Jim Maddox

All rights reserved.

Table of Contents

Prologue……………………………………………………………..4

Chapter 1: Introduction…………………………..……...5

Chapter 2: Who is God?………………………....……………12

Chapter 3: Heaven and Death………………...…..………29

Chapter 4: Why? The Lighter Side of Life…………....…39

Chapter 5: Grownups………………………………………..53

Chapter 6: Everyday Life…………………………...…………67

Epilogue………………………………………………..………..90

Prologue

There are no illustrations in this book and that is intentional. I encourage you to insert your own. Paste in what your children have drawn that is displayed on the refrigerator; ask them to contribute to your reflection journal and create original artwork around what you are journaling about. Add your own sketches. Add your own questions from life. Make this your own book, about your own questions.

Chapter 1

Introduction

They say that life is what happens while we're busy making plans. Much of the heart of life comes about unexpectedly, unplanned and, as is often the case, unexplained. In the midst of all the activity and the hurrying about, are our children. They take in all of life with wide-eyed wonderment and curiosity and constantly challenge us. What follows is an attempt to describe and share comments and questions I've received from my four children over the last 18 years. It is a journey of life through the eyes of 5 year olds as they ponder some very deep questions, such as "If God made us, who made God?" or "Why did your dad die so young?" and at the same time remind us of the playfulness of life with some not-so -deep questions like "When will Daddy be done with his job?" and "Could Jesus make a dog fly?".

What follows are philosophical questions that are as old as

humankind (Who made us? Who is God?) and as off-the-wall as they come ("Would it hurt if spaceship hit me in the face?"). All in all, what is compiled here is what our children's questions can teach us about life.

> Jesus asked 173 questions; he asked far more questions than he had asked of him.
>
> WHAT ARE THE QUESTIONS IN YOUR LIFE?

REFLECTIONS

1. What spoke to you in this section?

2. When have you been surprised this past week by others' observations or questions?

3. Really listen this week to those little ones around you. What questions do they raise that can teach you something or cause you to think or feel more deeply?

4. What are your questions that you asked this week?

5. What questions did you ask yourself as you reflected upon that Jesus asked far more questions than he provided answers?

6. What questions were asked of you this week?

Chapter 2

Who is God?

Who is God? When you consider that humans have been pondering this question since the beginning of time, is it any wonder that our children wrestle with this same deep concern? Many of our children's questions and comments are reflections of their environment, how they mirror their parents, their grandparents, and their Sunday school teachers. Many show a deeper philosophical issue, many that we can not answer, many without answers, many with complex answers, and many that call upon faith. Other questions remind us that children are not just little adults, but they see the world in their own unique way, simplistic, quirky, and yet often times profound.

"If Jesus made all of us, who made Jesus?" (Michael, age 4)

I think this question strikes at the heart of what people have asked for thousands of years. If God made everything, who made God? To respond to Michael's question with an answer that God made us, and that Jesus was born as a man, both fully human and fully God, would be to side step the real concern that Michael was raising. His question really shows a child's logical attempt to solve the issue of how did everything really begin (the concept of a first cause). This was really a profound moment to discuss with Michael that this is part of what makes God God; that God is "Who is;" God is the beginning.

> God said to Moses, "I AM WHO I AM. This is what you are to say to the Israelites: 'I AM has sent me to you.' "
> Exodus 3:14

One October afternoon, Kate, age 3, said, "David's birthday is next, right Daddy? Then it's your birthday and Jesus' birthday, right? What should we get Jesus for his birthday? He likes ballerinas." For Kate, Jesus is as real and close as her Mom and

Dad and he would obviously like what she likes. What should we get Jesus for his birthday?

> On coming to the house, they saw the child with his mother Mary, and they bowed down and worshiped him. Then they opened their treasures and presented him with gifts of gold and of incense and of myrrh.
> Matthew 2:11

Everyone knows three year olds get excited about birthdays. Children count down the days until their birthday. They anxiously await not only their next birthday but everyone around them. They even play "pretend birthday parties." They get excited about theirs, their brothers and sisters, mom and dad's, and even Jesus'. This, to me, is what Jesus meant when He said we must become like children. Jesus held a special closeness to children and I think this comment from Kate shows why. Her asking what should we get Jesus for His birthday illustrates the personal relationship with Jesus we as adults struggle to obtain. To a three year old, the personal relationship is simple and unemcumbered, without the limitations we as grownups place on God.

> And he said: "I tell you the truth, unless you change and become like little children, you will never enter the kingdom of heaven.
> Matthew 18:3

The child's personal identification with Jesus is also brought to life in Kate's answer to her own question. Kate's assertion that "He likes ballerinas" not only elicits comments from adults like, "Oh, isn't that sweet," but again shows the one-to-one relationship with Jesus so many of us long for. Kate's final comments on the subject were, "God made my arms. God my buddy. He like me."

The kids and I went to the Book Fair at school one Sunday afternoon. When we came home, Mom asked how it was. Kate (age 3) said excitedly, "I talked to God." David (age 5) pointed out that we saw Fr. Vasa! What this conversation taught my wife and I was that we too should be excited at the thought of talking with God. After all, isn't this the concept of prayer? Didn't Jesus say, "Where two or more of you are gathered in my name, I am there also?"

> If you believe, you will receive whatever you ask for in prayer."
>
> Matthew 21:22

David (age 4) asked Dad, "Could Jesus make a dog fly?" A parent's first reaction to this type of question is either to laugh or to comment that the question is really silly. What David was asking teaches us that Jesus could indeed make a dog fly (whether a little chihuahua or a wooly English sheepdog). There are no limits to what God can do, despite our continued efforts to place limits on Him. I think we tend to see limitations in ourselves and in others, in our relationships, and in our communities, and we have a hard time envisioning a God without limits. When a child asks what seems like an absurd question, it's an opportunity to grasp God's omnipotent /infinite powers.

Approaching Christmas, David (age 11) was talking to Jake (age 4) about being nice. David said, "Remember,

Santa's always watching." Jacob replied, "No he isn't.

He isn't God."

> Do not be terrified by them, for the LORD your God, who is among you, is a great and awesome God.
> Deuteronomy 7:21

Jake (age 6) when I asked him what he wanted for Christmas (this was early December, 2001), he responded, "I just want everyone in the world to be nice to each other." I think he had caught bits and pieces of our discussions of 9/11. Jake, I think God agrees with you and at your young age of 6, reflect the true spirit of Christmas and the most optimistic of hopes for "Peace on earth and goodwill towards men."

> Blessed are the peacemakers, for they will be called sons of God.
> Matthew 5:9

David, age 4, asked, "Were mice here when there were cavemen or dinosaurs or Jesus? When did they come?"

> In the beginning God created the heavens and the earth. Now the earth was formless and empty, darkness was over the surface of the deep, and the Spirit of God was hovering over the waters.
>
> Genesis 1:1-2

As a view of history or sequence of events, the Bible provides some insights. However, the Bible is not helpful in many instances involving science and evolution. This is why I like so much – Rich Mullins' (former singer, song writer, and ragamuffin) quote on why we read the Bible – "We read the Bible not to find the truth but to find God."

Michael, at age 3, asked, "How did Jesus make us? How did he get the skin on us? Did he use glue to keep our legs on"? Call Jesus on the phone so I can tell him thank you for my legs and feet and arms." Believe it or not, these were the actual questions Michael raised, all in one breath! His mental wheels were spinning at hyper speed! These types of spiritual questions are very important to children and show us grownups the true beauty of procreation. Michael's request to call Jesus on the phone and personally thank Him helps remind us that we thank God for our very being but also reinforces the fact that we don't even need a telephone to talk with Jesus. A telephone is used to communicate with someone who we cannot be with at that time.

While saying prayers at night, David said, "Thank you for everything except the devil." Kids can definitely teach us about good and evil, and yes, we should thank God for everything,

I remember at age 4 Kate making the comment, "God was busy when he put us together. It took a lot of work." Kids remind us of how awesome God is and while God's ability is limitless, we can marvel at all that we have been given, and yes, in the eyes of a 4 year old (and a 50 year old), it would appear to be a lot of work!

Michael (age 4) and David (age 3) were playing Mass in the playroom. Michael was the priest. He was talking loud gibberish (what he understands the priest to be saying). They were singing in chant. They were using a little white table as the altar and four chairs as a pew. David was the guitarist. Michael laughed out of embarrassment when Carol looked into the playroom. David said, "Priest no laugh, just talk." Michael made the sign of the cross and said, "Christ the Lord forgive your sins. Peace be with you." We can learn a tremendous amount about ourselves and our culture by watching our children at play. Their words and actions are a mirror into what we value, where we spend our time, and most importantly, what they are absorbing and internalizing.

REFLECTIONS

1. What spoke to you in this section?

2. When have you been surprised this past week by other's observations or questions?

3. Really listen this week to those little ones around you. What questions to they raise that can teach you something or cause you to think or feel more deeply?

4. What are your questions that you asked this week?

5. What questions did you ask yourself as you reflected upon the relevant scripture passages?

6. Who do you say God is?

7. What should your gift be to Jesus for his birthday?

8. How would you characterize your personal relationship with God?

9. Do you believe God likes you?

10. Do you talk with God?

11. How do you view prayer?

12. Have you placed any limits on God?

13. Where have you placed limiting beliefs in your own life?

14. What are you truly thankful for that you have not considered in the past?

15. What were your words and actions this week mirroring?

16. What did you value this week?

17. What do you believe God's greatest gift to humanity was/is?

Chapter 3

Heaven and Death

> By the sweat of your brow you will eat your food until you return to the ground, since from it you were taken; for dust you are and to dust you will return."
> Genesis 3:19

When Michael was 7 he had this question for Carol: "Mommy, after we die, will they put our bones in a museum?" What seems like an automatic "No, of course not," this question seems quite logical after considering what you find in museums. Michael's real concern, however, is what happens to our bodies after this thing called death.

> Now we know that if the earthly tent we live in is destroyed, we have a building from God, an eternal house in heaven, not built by human hands.
> 2 Corinthians 5:1

Kate, at age 4, declared, "I am so excited to go to heaven someday." A simple reminder again from someone of simple, trusting faith. Yes, we too should truly be excited to go to heaven. Kate's major concern with death and going to heaven at age 3 was, "Will God have a car seat for me in heaven?" This question made her Mom cry.

Michael (age 4) said this to David (age 2) at lunch while eating Jell-O. "When I grow up and Mommy and Daddy die and I make the Jell-O - I'm going to put sour cream in the Jell-O and then throw it in your face." A lighter side to death, but it's really about rules and an ability to control our environment. It's about wanting to have some control and to be in charge.

Michael (age 6) asked, "What will happen if the earth

gets too crowded, if God makes too many people?" We discussed how Jesus makes babies and they are born into the world and how Jesus also calls people to live with him in heaven. A natural response to our view of limited resources and our scarcity mentality. Then he asked if heaven could get too crowded. We decided that God plans things out perfectly and that heaven could never be too crowded. There's always room for more.

At a lunchtime discussion: "Why can't we call Jesus on the phone." Mom said that because he's in our hearts and in heaven, we don't need phones to talk to him. We can pray to him anytime.

Pray continually.

1 Thessalonians 5:17

One day the kids were asking questions about who do you know in heaven, and the death of grandparents entered into the discussion. Mom said "Nanny is with God and Daddy's Daddy, too. Won't that be great to see them all someday?" The boys said, "Yea! That will be great! The kids were clearly excited about this reunion.

REFLECTIONS

1. What spoke to you in this section?

2. When have you been surprised this past week by other's observations or questions?

3. Really listen this week to those little ones around you. What questions to they raise that can teach you something or cause you to think or feel more deeply?

4. What are your questions that you asked this week?

5. What questions did you ask yourself as you reflected upon the relevant scripture passages?

6. What is your view of death?

7. What questions do you have about death?

8. What areas of your life do you wish you had more control over?

9. Do you view life as one of abundance and possibilities or one of scarcity and limited responses and limited opportunities?

Chapter 4

Why? The Lighter Side of Life

> There is a time for everything,
> and a season for every activity under the heavens:
>
> a time to be born and a time to die,
> a time to plant and a time to uproot,
>
> a time to kill and a time to heal,
> a time to tear down and a time to build,
>
> a time to weep and a time to laugh,
> a time to mourn and a time to dance,
>
> a time to scatter stones and a time to gather them,
> a time to embrace and a time to refrain from embracing,
>
> a time to search and a time to give up,
> a time to keep and a time to throw away,
>
> a time to tear and a time to mend,
> a time to be silent and a time to speak,
>
> a time to love and a time to hate,
> a time for war and a time for peace.
>
> Ecclesiastes 3-8

While some of the questions our children pose are about

life's deep questions, many other questions just come out of left field and are hard to categorize. Across this whole spectrum, they evoke a smile and help us to appreciate the sense of humor in our children. There truly is a time for everything, especially laughter.

Like Art Linkletter said, kids do say the darnest things. What follows are questions and comments that range from the sweet to the not-so sweet and from logical ideas to the truly bizarre.

Michael - age 5

"Do locusts always park their shells on trees?"

Seems logical, and the apparent scientific answer is <u>Yes</u>.

Jake – age 3

Carol asked Jake how he was getting so much taller; how do you do that? Jake's response was, "Well Mom, there's this machine at this place that makes you go up and down and that's how I got taller."

Almost sounds like he was describing the ancient rack????

I'm not sure that we knew the original intent of the device during medival times!

Michael - age 5

"I'm going to take the seeds from his orange so we won't have to buy more fruit at the store - and buy a cow so we won't run out of milk." This is quite advanced economics. Theory in action. Many adults would be wise to heed this same path. (Is it a coincidence that Michael went on to major in business in college?)

Michael (age 5) and David (age 4) were talking with me about Michael's first day of preschool: David asked about school and I told him that next year he would get to go. Michael responded, "and then I will get to stay home." This seems very logical. We teach children to take turns and this to a child is a rational extension of "taking turns."

Made up jokes by Jake (age 6): Question: What do you get when you take the word STOP off of a stop sign?

Answer: "A red sign on a post"

Question: "What do you get when you put a pogo stick in the back of a pick up truck?"

Answer: "A pogo pick up truck"

David (age 4) asked, "How did the cave men cut their birthday cakes if knives weren't invented yet?" What a great conversation starter. It is these type of questions that can engage us in profound philosophical discussions for hours.

David (age 5) asked, "What would happen if I fell and part of my skull came off?" I would have been concerned and comforting David when he asked this, but he was not asking it out of fear. Instead, it was a detached, just wondering type of question.

David (age 5) wanted to go to someone's house from his preschool. He said, "I can't remember their address, but I know it has some numbers in it."

This to David seemed to be more than enough information.

David (age 4) and Michael (age 6) were talking to our babysitter and asking about her sister (whom they didn't even know). Michael asked what kind of car she drove and Amy told them. David said, "I think I've seen her but didn't realize it was your sister."

David (age 3) said, "Daddy, you won't recognize the station wagon." I said, "Why, what's different?" David said, "Different is not the same. Ask a literal question and you sometimes get a literal answer.

At lunch Carol, Michael (age 5) and David (age 4) were having a very interesting conversation about the devil. (Michael had questions from what was discussed in Kindergarten). The conversation just kept rolling along for about 10 minutes and Carol just tried to keep answering as fast as the discussion was going. Both boys were asking non-stop questions and it was a very engaging conversation (on the level of 4 and 5 year olds!) Carol thought they were very deep into the discussion when David had something to say. While listening with anticipation for his next comment or question, David said, "Mommy, when I get a lot of Jell-O in my mouth it tastes like Jell-O juice." I guess that meant we were finished with our theological discussion. I think we as adults often reach our limit with deep conversations and have our train of thought shift; David just didn't have a filter yet to avoid asking the question out loud!

Peeling cornbread off of a corndog, Michael (age 4) said he was taking the wool off of the sheep. Carol asked him what he will do with the wool. He said he would make a sweater.

A friend was over at our house and asked Michael (age 5) and David (age 4) about the deer head mounted on our wall. David said, "Daddy shot 'em and we ate his body and then put his face on the wall." This pretty much sums up big game hunting and taxidermy in one, easy, straightforward statement.

David (age 5):"Would you get your name in the paper if you jumped off the Sears' Tower?" We had just visited Chicago and the kids were impressed that after asking so many times, "Is that the tallest building in the world?" and being told no; finally when asking at the Sears Tower, the answer was affirmative.

I asked David (age 4) if he wanted a little of Kate's toast. He said, "No thanks. I'm sick enough as it is."

David (age 3) asked, "Would it hurt if a spaceship hit you in the face?"

I came home from work and I asked David (age 4) what he did today. He said, "I changed my body." It's this type of response that leaves parent scratching their heads. I didn't even know how to respond!

David (age 4) said, "Hey Daddy. Do you want to hear how it sounds when I throw-up?" (This was followed by convincing sound effects.)

REFLECTIONS

1. What spoke to you in this section?

2. When have you been surprised this past week by other's observations or questions?

3. Really listen this week to those little ones around you. What questions to they raise that can teach you something or cause you to think or feel more deeply?

4. What are your questions that you asked this week?

5. What questions did you ask yourself as you reflected upon the relevant scripture passages?

6. What has made you laugh this week?

7. What interesting or off the wall questions did you ask this week?

8. What questions were you asked this week that made you smile or say, "huh?"

Chapter 5

Grownups

> When I was a child, I talked like a child, I thought like a child, I reasoned like a child. When I became a man, I put the ways of childhood behind me. 12 For now we see only a reflection as in a mirror; then we shall see face to face. Now I know in part; then I shall know fully, even as I am fully known.
>
> 1 Corinthians 13

Much of what our kids discuss and ask questions about are reflections of the life we lead as grown-ups (or "grumps" for short as we sometimes have been aptly called.) They offer us a unique perspective into the lives we lead and give us an interesting and fresh perspective on what grown-ups are really all about.

Carol was driving Michael (age 7) and David (age 6) to school. Michael asked David, "What are you going to be when you grow-up?" David said, "I'm not gonna tell. You have to wait 'til I'm grown-up and find me in my uniform and then you'll know."

Daddy told Kate (age 5), "I like taking care of you." Kate responded, "Of course you do. Grown-ups always like taking care of their children."

Such trusting faith. A simple assumption; one that should be a universal truth. But the harsh reality is that grown-ups don't always like taking care of their children, but the children depend upon us completely. We learned this first hand when we did foster care and saw the abuse in the children we cared for. This had a great impact on our kids.

Michael (age 5) asked how much a toy was that he saw in a catalog. I said, "39.90." He said, "Is that a lot of money?" I said, "It's quite a bit." Then he asked, "Will that use all of our money?"

Michael said, "What will we do with our toys when we are grown-ups?" A profound question; one that begs us to remain young and surrounded by the carefree time of youth, playtime and toys. Children look at adults and they obviously recognize a lack of "toys" and so often see instead the drudgery of "work."

Jacob (age 5) after completing his first week of all-day Kindergarten, said, "I missed my toys. How much more school do I have?" Beginning the journey!

Jacob (age 3) refers to Kellogg (the main highway across town) as the "Basketball Road". We have driven it so much for practices and games that's what he associates it with. Whenever we go over to the east side of the city without the older kids, Jacob would ask, "Why are we going on the "Basketball road?"

Michael (age 6) asked David (age 5), "Do you think Mommy will <u>make</u> us fold our clothes?" David said, "No, 'cuz that would be "slaving." View of fairness and equality – even at a young age.

After giving them a new activity book in the car, David (age 4) asked, "How come we didn't get more than one?" Mom said, "I thought you were old enough to share." David said, "Well, we're not." Assumptions that we make about our children.

When asked what he wanted to be when he grows up, Jake (age 3) replied, "I want to be a baby."

Jake (age 3) while watching old home movies saw Kate (who was 8 at the time) when she was just 2, said, "Kate, make yourself little again." This made Mom cry. It is apparent that our kids were quite skilled at making Mom cry, without even trying!

Most of life allows u-turns and God gives us many second and third (and often forth) chances; but going back to being younger is not one of those options. It makes us reflect, and as we get older we begin to see what our own parents used to say about how fast time goes by. Our own children remind us how fleeting childhood really is and what a short time we have with them as small wonders of God. Like many things in life though, we often don't realize how short this time is until it is past.

Jake and Kate have many possible options available to them in this marvelous life, but being little again is not one of them.

David (age 6) asked Mom, "When will Daddy be done with his job?" Our children are good reminders of our priorities and the fact that we can get wrapped up in our jobs and careers. Work. Life. Balance.

Jim was preparing to mow. He asked Michael (age 5) if he wanted to help pick up the sticks. Michael's response was, "That's not my job." (Needless to say, he picked up the sticks.) What a grown-up response! We've heard it a lot in corporate America but not from a 5 year old. Maybe now we know where adults get it from.

Michael (age 7) asked, "Mommy, do you and Daddy want another baby? Are you having trouble?" Little ears hear many unintended conversations.

David (age 4) asked, "Daddy, when you were a baby, were there no sound effects?" It's these types of questions from our kids that make us feel _really,_ I mean _really_ old.

Jacob (age 4) asked Mom, "When will I be done being

me? I am ready to grow up; will I still be Jake when I'm bigger Mommy?" Carol said, "yes". Jake responded with , "No, I'm done being me."

We had a discussion on Michael Jordan retiring from basketball. (We described his retirement by saying he's done playing basketball on TV. He wants to be something else now,) Three days before Halloween, David (age 5) told me he didn't want to be a cowboy anymore. (He wore the costume to Preschool.) He wanted to be a paleontologist or Robin Hood or Superman because he "retired" from being a cowboy. He already did that. Now he wants to be something else.

Kate (age 4) said, "I can watch R movies when I grow up because I'm going to be a Mommy."

Kids don't like being told no and even worse, they don't like to wait. We tell our kids, "Not until you're grown. For Kate, being a Mommy equals being a grown-up, and of course, R movies are only for grown-ups.

Michael (age 6) asked, "Daddy, when you get your Ph.D., can you change jobs?" When I told him yes he said, "Good because I want you to be a race car driver."

David (age 5) was playing restaurant.

"What would you like to order?"

Mom said, "What's the special?"

David answered, "Chinese and chicken fried bananas."

Mommy said, "Sounds interesting. I'll order that."

David calling to the kitchen said, "Order up please, Charlie."

At supper, David (age 5) said, "I've got 2 jobs. I can read your mind, Daddy." Daddy said, "You can?" David said, "Yep, that's my job." Daddy said, "What am I thinking?" David said, "I can't tell you. It's a secret." My other job is to keep it secret and if I tell you they'll take away my second job."

Children can have a very well developed sense of humor and can use logic to convey their stories. By the way, Carol and the other kids never did find out what I was thinking. I helped David keep his secret.

REFLECTIONS

1. What spoke to you in this section?

2. When have you been surprised this past week by other's observations or questions?

3. Really listen this week to those little ones around you. What questions to they raise that can teach you something or cause you to think or feel more deeply?

4. What are your questions that you asked this week?

5. What questions did you ask yourself as you reflected upon the relevant scripture passages?

6. What did you want to be when you grew up?

7. What are your fondest memories of growing up?

8. What has shaped your narrative as a grown-up?

9. Are you good at keeping secrets? What secrets have you kept?

Chapter 6

Everyday Life

Are you enjoying the ride?

On the way to Kansas City on vacation, Michael (age 7) was sitting in the front seat just watching the road. Carol asked him what he was doing. He said, "Nothing, just enjoying the ride."

It appears that at the tender age of 7, Michael has life figured out. Many adults have not figured out either how to enjoy the ride or the value of taking this approach to life.

We can certainly learn from this simple, straight forward response. We as adults should spend more time doing "nothing" and simply enjoy the ride. We need to enjoy each moment and not strive to constantly be busy. This is a challenge when our culture values "doing" over "being."

> ## "Be still and know that I am God"
>
> Psalm 46: 10

On another family road trip, Jake (age 3) shared a reflection on our trip home from the Grand Canyon. David (age 10) asked him if he was going to take a nap. Jake responded, "I don't like to take a nap cause I don't know what's happening."

> Then he returned to his disciples and found them sleeping. "Couldn't you men keep watch with me for one hour?" he asked Peter. "Watch and pray so that you will not fall into temptation. The spirit is willing, but the flesh is weak."
>
> Matthew 25:40-41

David (age 5): When asked what he wanted for lunch, David replied, "A cheeseburger and a cup of mud." Ok, no deep insights here, but certainly a reflection of something he picked up about coffee. Interestingly we were not coffee drinkers nor did we frequent cheap diners!

Kate (age 2) asks, "Do you like me?" which is immediately answered with hugs and kisses. She asked this question a lot as a 2 year old. I think she was realizing what we all inquire from those we are connected to. We all seek reassurance and even though we know we are loved, liked, and cared for, we still need verbal and physical affirmation.

> Again Jesus said, "Simon son of John, do you love me?"
> John 21:16

Carol was taking chocolate chip cookies out of the oven. Kate (age 3) said, "Daddy, I want a cookie." Carol said, "After supper." Kate said, "I'm talking to Daddy."

Anyone who has had children knows how they work the system and realize there are two parents from which their "needs" can be met.

I'm sure this is a reflection of different roles we play as

parents; and yes, Carol is the disciplinarian and the sane one and I'm the overgrown playmate and creator of fun experiences. All roles are necessary.

Mom asked Jake (age 3) if he had broken the little toy he was holding (it was in 2 pieces!). Jake said, "I don't know, possibly." Even as a 3 year old, Jake understood and approached an issue of personal accountability with hesitation and contemplation. He didn't offer denial. What he offered was possibility and uncertainty. Insightful!

The day before Carol's birthday, after the kids and Jim just came back from "birthday shopping," David (age 5) came running out to Carol from the bedroom where the wrapping was going on and said in a whisper, "We got you an exercise video, but it's a secret." David understood the excitement of the moment and wanted to share with his Mom. We as adults often want to, even feel compelled to, share our secrets. They just seem to burst from us at times, and yet there is something critical and essential in the keeping of important secrets that have been entrusted to us.

> A gossip betrays a confidence, but a trustworthy person keeps a secret.
>
> Proverbs 11:13

David (age 5) and Kate (age 3) were talking. David told Kate she couldn't go to the store after supper. She started crying and said, "David said I can't go." Jim told Kate that she didn't have to listen to him." She said, between sobs, "But I am."

It's easy for adults to give a simple solution, such as, "Just don't listen to him." How often as adults, when being hurt by another person and told not to let it bother you, just want to respond, "But it does."

Daddy was looking at a magazine and Kate (age 3) saw a picture of a teddy bear. Daddy asked Kate if she wanted to read the magazine. Kate replied, "Well, I don't know how to read, but I can look at the pictures." When have we responded to our potential limitations with our potential opportunities? We often only see what we can't do and don't take the next step to explore and identify what we can do.

While fixing supper, Daddy gave David (age 4) a hug and said, "I missed you today." David hugged Daddy back and said, "I missed you too, big guy!"

Waiting for Michael (age 3) to try to hit the ball again

during our indoor "baseball game," he was taking off his hat and rubbing his head. I asked him if he was ok. He responded, "Yea, I'm just unsweating."

The morning after getting a buzz haircut for the summer, I asked Jake, age 3, if he liked it. He said, "Yea, put it back on now." We as adults often respond this way to change. We like it for its novelty and in the short term, but want to go back to our old way; that which is comfortable and familiar. But just like Jake's hair, we really can't go back to the way things were. Life flows and moves in one direction.

David (age 4) wanted me to get a game out for him. I said, "How about Stretch Out Sam?" He said, "Well, it's a possibility."

Yes, life is truly full of possibilities.

Michael (age 5) was watching Mom try to cook and help David (age 4) and Kate (age 2) and he said, "Looks like you got your hands full."

How observant! Yes, parents (especially young Moms) not only appear to have their hands full but can be overwhelmed. But as Mae West said, "Too much of a good thing is wonderful."

Michael and David were "camping" on the patio. Michael wanted Carol to come and see them. He phrased it, "Join us, Mommy!" We want to share our experiences. We want others to join us. We want others to experience what we are experiencing.

> From him the whole body, joined and held together by every supporting ligament, grows and builds itself up in love, as each part does its work.
>
> Ephesians 4:16

Getting Michael's (age 5) snack cup ready. Mom said she would fill it with some good things and began putting in some crackers. As he was going outside to wait he said, "You are so sweet." What a sense of gratitude and affirmation, spoken from the heart.

David (age 5) said, "Daddy, would you share your cookie if you had one?" I said, "Of course." He paused and said, "Daddy, you need a cookie, don't you?"

Any adult who has to negotiate can learn from this line of reasoning. David should make a great attorney!

David (age 4) had the following conversation with Mom while she was cutting his hair:

David: "I hate girls."

Carol: "You mean you don't like me."

David: "Well, I mean I don't like their attitude."

We often are put off by others attitudes.

> Get rid of all bitterness, rage and anger, brawling and slander, along with every form of malice. Be kind and compassionate to one another, forgiving each other, just as in Christ God forgave you.
> Ephesians 4:31-32

Jake (age 3) while camping at the Grand Canyon, fell in the tent and hit his head. Michael (age 11), asked him if he wanted him to kiss his head. Jake said, "No, it's just a dent." This makes me laugh and I can't help but think about the Black Knight from Monty Python and the Holy Grail who said, "It's only a flesh wound."

Continuing this loving relationship between siblings, on the same camp out, Michael was laying down in the tent and Jake asked him if he was eating a cookie. Michael said, "No." So Jake crammed one in his mouth. Michael complained to mom and Jake said, "It was just a joke." We know that saying something was just a joke does not undo the hurt or insult, but even as adults we use this phrase (which I'm sure is where he heard it from).

Michael (age 3) said, "I want hot dogs and mashed potatoes because that is what is in my heart."

What is in your heart?

Jake (age 6) at supper, said, "I ate a whole piece of tomato and I didn't even make a yucky face or throw-up." Can you guess he doesn't like tomatoes? It's amazing what we are capable of enduring and even have a sense of accomplishment when we do endure something necessary but less than desirable.

Watching David (age 5) in the bathroom, Daddy asked if he had washed his hands. (David had just entered the bathroom.) David said, "Yep!" Daddy said, "You did not!" David said, "I did too you doubting Mustafa!" Yes, our children watched Disney movies growing up, obviously a reflection of their culture!

When Daddy came home from work, David (age 5) said, "I went to the library at school today." Kate (age 3) said, "I went to the library too. NOT!"

Putting on a puppet show, David (age 3) asked Carol what

animal she liked the best. She thought David meant which animal puppet so she started saying how she liked each of them. After she had finished he said, "Mommy, that is not the question! Which animal do you like at the zoo!" He was wanting to know which animal from the zoo to pretend his puppet was. We often get the wrong answer because the question others are hearing is not the same as the question we thought we were asking.

What question do you most want answered?

Kate (age 5) was having a discussion with Dad about the blizzard we were having that day. Kate said, "Blisters are really cold, right Daddy?" I said, "Well, I'm not sure blisters are cold, but sometimes they hurt." Kate said, "Why do blisters hurt? Why would the blister outside hurt?" Kate's understanding of blizzards as a word didn't register, but she thought she heard the word blister, or perhaps my pronunciation of the word blizzard sounded like blister, or perhaps she was, in fact, saying blizzard – but I was hearing blister… Is it any wonder we have miscommunications? It's interesting when we have conversations where each person is coming from a completely different perspective.

While on vacation we stopped to see the Arch in St. Louis. Michael (age 6) said, "I'm tired of walking. Can't we just see stuff from the car?" Spoken like a true kid!

While Dad was throwing a curve ball to David (age 6) with a wiffle ball, David said, "Throw me something I can hit. I'm only a little kid."

Life often throws us (both adults and children) curveballs. We often say to God, "throw me something I can hit, I'm only (age - young/old, blind, hard of hearing, tired, etc...). (Fill in the blank for yourself.)

Take time to listen to your children. We have so much to learn from them. Despite their apparent limited knowledge, they are full of wisdom. They challenge our assumptions and push us to try new things. They reinforce our faith (often weak) about the goodness of God. They make us laugh. They touch our hearts. They are mirrors of ourselves and yet each is a unique individual. They teach us about our values and our beliefs through their probing questions and insightful responses. But most of all, they teach us about the goodness of life; that we are (fully) and wonderfully made and that we are deeply loved by God.

> I praise you because I am fearfully and wonderfully made; your works are wonderful, I know that full well.
> Psalm 139:14

REFLECTIONS

1. What spoke to you in this section?

2. When have you been surprised this past week by other's observations or questions?

3. Really listen this week to those little ones around you. What questions to they raise that can teach you something or cause you to think or feel more deeply?

4. What are your questions that you asked this week?

5. What questions did you ask yourself as you reflected upon the relevant scripture passages?

6. In what ways did you take time this week to "enjoy the ride?"

7. How can you incorporate "doing nothing" into your day?

8. Were you awake this week? Did you take in your surroundings? Did you know what was happening?

9. Have you given affirmation to those who need it this week?

10. In what ways have you been shown "you are liked" this week?

11. How do you embrace possibilities and uncertainity this week?

12. What have you really listened to this week?

13. Where have you seen possibilities this week beyond apparent limitations?

Epilogue

Someone close to me reviewed this manuscript and shared that it needed an ending. They wanted me to tell my story, why I collected all the comments, where I am now, how it feels to have grown children, and what is their reaction to this book. I have struggled deeply with even attempting to answer these questions. This book was one of the most joyous and at the same time one of the most emotionally difficult undertakings. The last comment from my kids is almost 14 years old at the completion of this project. I have always been sentimental, I overthink things, I ask a lot of questions and I struggle at my core to still believe in God and Jesus. The collection of questions my kids asked started out with no bigger intention, other than just writing them down on scraps of paper or post-it notes and throwing them in a kitchen drawer. At the end of the year, we included them in our Christmas letter to family and friends. After several years, one old friend suggested the comments be compiled into a book, with the question my daughter asked about her carseat, as the title, and a profound journey began.

Today, my kids are grown and have done some amazing things and have had some great adventures of their own. The oldest three have graduated college and are on their own. The youngest is a Junior in college and studying philosophy and anthropology (which makes sense with the questions he has always asked.) They are each navigating life in their own unique way. Their mom and I are no longer married (after 28 years), as of 4 years ago. Just like many of the questions our kids ask, somethings have no answers.

Embrace all life has to offer, the joys, the hurts, the disappointments, the mysteries, and beauty of every moment we are given.

Go and write your own epilogue, write your own story; ask your own questions; and live your own story.

www.ingramcontent.com/pod-product-compliance
Lightning Source LLC
Chambersburg PA
CBHW061459040426
42450CB00008B/1422